CALLING ALL INNOVATORS

A CAREER FOR YOU

AIR TRAVEL

SCIENCE · TECHNOLOGY · ENGINEERING

BY STEVEN OTFINOSKI

CHILDREN'S PRESS®

An Imprint of Scholastic Inc.
New York Toronto London Auckland Sydney
Mexico City New Delhi Hong Kong
Danbury, Connecticut

CONTENT CONSULTANT
Jacob Zeiger, EDC Liaison Engineer, The Boeing Company, Everett, Washington

PHOTOGRAPHS ©: age fotostock: 29 (Jochen Tack/imageBroker), 37 (Ton Koene); Alamy Images: 30 bottom (Aerial Archives), 5 left, 53 (Alan Payton), 59 bottom right (Antony Nettle), 56 (Charles Polidano/Touch The Skies), 13 top (Courtesy: CSU Archives/Everett Collection), 43 center (David Coleman), 58 top (Dennis Hallinan), 27 top (epa european pressphoto agency b.v), 48 (Erik Tham), 15 (Everett Collection), 10 (GL Archive), 6, 8 (Hilary Morgan), 3, 28, 32 (Jack Sullivan), 31, 40, 43 top (Jeff Greenberg), 19 bottom (Mary Evans Picture Library), 58 bottom, 59 bottom left (NASA Photo), 36 (Norbert Michalke/imageBroker), 30 top (Peter Titmuss), 42 (PF-(sdasm2)), 21 (Piers Cavendish/Imagestate Media Partners Limited - Impact Photos), 43 bottom (SFL Travel), 4 left, 11, 12 (SZ Photo/Scher/DIZ Muenchen GmbH, Sueddeutsche Zeitung Photo), 18 top (Trinity Mirror/Mirrorpix), 45, 51 (Zuma Press); AP Images: 26 (Press Association), 55 top; Boeing Images: 39; Corbis Images: 13 bottom (Bettmann), 4 right, 22 (John Zich/zrlmages), 9 (Minnesota Historical Society); Getty Images: 19 top (Ami Vitale), 20 (Bill Foley/The LIFE Images Collection), 27 bottom, 44 (Bloomberg), 59 top (Carl De Souza/AFP), 16 (Chicago History Museum), 57 (Gary Conner), 17 (John McGrail/The LIFE Images Collection), 54 bottom (Joshua Roberts/Bloomberg), 54 top (Karl Schumacher/The LIFE Images Collection), 18 bottom (Keystone-France/Gamma-Keystone), 50 right (Mark Wilson), 24 (Tim Boyle); Media Bakery: 34 (IMG100), 41 (Monty Rakusen), 33 (Thierry Foulon), 25 (WESTEND61); Newscom/Chris Sweda/MCT: 49; PhotoEdit/Chris Smith: 50 left; Rex USA/Reso: 52; Science Source: 5 right, 46 (Mark D. Phillips), 14 (Photo Researchers, Inc.), 55 bottom (RIA Novosti); U.S. Navy/Mass Communication Specialist 2nd Class Oscar Espinoza: cover.

LIBRARY OF CONGRESS CATALOGING-IN-PUBLICATION DATA
Otfinoski, Steven, author.
  Air travel : science, technology, and engineering / by Steven Otfinoski.
      pages cm. — (Calling all innovators: a career for you)
  Summary: "Learn about the history of air travel and find out what it takes to make it in this exciting career field" — Provided by publisher.
  Audience: Age 9–12.
  Audience: Grades 4–6.
  Includes bibliographical references and index.
  ISBN 978-0-531-20538-9 (library binding : alk. paper) — ISBN 978-0-531-21174-8 (pbk. : alk. paper)
  1. Air travel — Juvenile literature. 2. Aeronautics — Vocational guidance — Juvenile literature. 3. Aeronautics — History — Juvenile literature. I. Title.
  TL720.084 2015
  629.13'0023 — dc23   2014030287

All rights reserved. Published in 2015 by Children's Press, an imprint of Scholastic Inc.
Printed in the United States of America 113

1 2 3 4 5 6 7 8 9 10 R 24 23 22 21 20 19 18 17 16 15

CALLING ALL INNOVATORS

A CAREER FOR YOU

Science, technology, engineering, arts, and math are the fields that drive innovation. Whether they are finding ways to make our lives easier or developing the latest entertainment, the people who work in these fields are changing the world for the better. Do you have what it takes to join the ranks of today's greatest innovators? Read on to discover whether air travel is a career for you.

TABLE *of* CONTENTS

Transcontinental Air Transport was one of the first airlines to offer trips across the United States.

An airport employee inspects a passenger's identification at a security checkpoint.

Flight attendants provide a variety of services to help make flying pleasant.

AN INTERVIEW WITH

An American Airlines flight takes off from New York City.

Brothers Wilbur and Orville Wright were
the first to build working airplanes.

CHAPTER ONE

LEARNING TO FLY

More than a century ago, humans conquered the skies with the first airplanes. Yet for decades afterward, the vast majority of Americans continued traveling to distant places by train, ship, or automobile. Air travel for the average person didn't become a reality until the 1950s. Today, millions of Americans travel by air each year for business, for pleasure, or to visit family and friends.

Why did commercial air travel take so long to catch on? What technological developments and historical events shaped the air travel industry? These and other questions will be answered as we take to the skies and explore the intriguing world of air travel.

AIRPLANE LANDMARKS

1927	1936	1952	1976
Lockheed Aircraft Company produces the Vega, a single-engine transport plane that can carry up to six passengers.	The twin-engine Douglas DC-3 makes its first passenger flights, carrying up to 21 passengers.	The de Havilland Comet from Great Britain becomes the world's first large commercial jet airliner.	France and Great Britain's Concorde, the first supersonic commercial jet, begins transatlantic passenger service.

THE BEGINNINGS OF AIR TRAVEL

The first commercial flight took place on January 1, 1914, just over
a decade after the Wright brothers first flew at Kitty Hawk, North
Carolina. Abram Phiel, the former mayor of St. Petersburg, Florida, was
the sole passenger in a two-seat Benoist XIV plane. The flight covered a
distance of 21 miles (34 kilometers) in 23 minutes and cost Phiel $400.

By the 1920s, well-to-do businessmen flew on such planes as
the Vega, a single-engine transport plane that could hold up to six
passengers and travel 500 miles (805 km) without refueling. But
even among the rich, plane travel was far surpassed by a different
aviation wonder—the dirigible, or airship. Airships consisted of a
large balloon filled with gas. A **gondola** that could carry passengers
and cargo hung beneath the balloon. Airships were invented in the
1850s in France. By the 1930s, they were far more popular than
airplanes for travel. They were more technically advanced and were
capable of crossing the Atlantic Ocean. They could also carry many
more passengers and were safer than airplanes.

An airship lands in England in 1918 after a journey across the Atlantic Ocean.

GAS-FILLED
BALLOON

R 34

GONDOLA

OPEN COCKPIT

MAIL LOADED INTO CLOTH BAGS

Aviator Charles Lindbergh (top right) loads airmail onto his plane in 1926.

GETTING THE MAIL THROUGH

At first, airplanes were mostly used to carry cargo, especially mail. In May 1918, the U.S. government began the world's first permanent airmail service. Small airmail companies popped up across the United States in the 1920s. Some mail planes also carried a few passengers along on flights, almost as an afterthought.

The Airmail Act of 1930 based government contracts with these companies on how much mail their aircraft could carry. This encouraged airline carriers to build or buy larger airplanes that could carry more mail and passengers to make each flight more profitable. As engines grew bigger and more powerful, planes were able to travel greater distances. Pan American Airways, established in 1927, held the exclusive mail route between the United States and Cuba. It eventually extended its territory to Mexico and other Latin American countries, making it a pioneer in flight between continents.

FLAMES CAUSED BY GASES INSIDE AIRSHIP

The Hindenburg *crash convinced many people that airplanes were a safer choice for travel than airships.*

AN ERA ENDS, ANOTHER BEGINS

The airship's supremacy in passenger air travel ended on May 6, 1937. That day, the German airship *Hindenburg* was about to land in Lakehurst, New Jersey, when it burst into flames. A spark had set fire to the highly flammable hydrogen gas that filled the ship. Some 36 people died. The crash made people believe airships were unsafe for air travel. Passengers quickly stopped using them.

Travelers began flying on airplanes, which had become more advanced with bigger engines, more space, and increased safety features. The most impressive of these planes was the Douglas DC-3, which boasted twin engines, could reach speeds of 170 miles per hour (274 kph), and could hold a maximum of 21 passengers. Other advancements in commercial planes in the 1930s included better radio equipment and pressurized **cabins** that allowed passengers to breathe more easily at high **altitudes**.

FLYING BOATS

Despite technological advances, long-distance flights, especially over oceans and seas, were a problem for transport planes. Plane engines still weren't powerful enough, and their tanks couldn't hold enough fuel to complete these long flights safely. The development of seaplanes called flying boats solved this problem. These large, multiengine airplanes could land on water when necessary. They didn't need runways, which were expensive to build. They were used not only for passenger flights but also for sea rescues and for patrolling waterways.

The first practical seaplane was built and flown by Glenn H. Curtiss in 1911. The German Dornier Do-X, first flown in 1929, was one of the earliest commercial flying boats. By the 1930s, flying boats reached the peak of their popularity. The Boeing 314 Clipper, one of the last of the flying boats to be developed, could carry up to 74 passengers.

A Boeing 314 flying boat takes off from water in 1941.

PROPELLERS HELP PLANE GAIN ENOUGH SPEED TO TAKE OFF

BOAT-LIKE UNDERSIDE HELPS PLANE FLOAT

FIRST THINGS FIRST

A TAT plane flies above the clouds in 1928.

THE RAILROAD PAVES THE WAY

While air travel gradually replaced rail travel for many people, early airlines relied heavily on railroads. The Transcontinental Air Transport (TAT) was one of the first airlines to offer trips across the United States. To do this, TAT relied on rail lines for part of the journey. By July 1929, TAT routes covered 2,000 miles (3,219 km) by air and 1,000 miles (1,609 km) by rail. Passengers flew from city to city, then boarded a train to take them to the next airport.

THE LINDBERGH LINE

TAT was an ambitious venture. It earned the endorsement of aviator Charles Lindbergh, who flew the first solo flight across the Atlantic from New York to Paris in 1927. TAT proudly called itself the Lindbergh Line. Lindbergh actually piloted part of the first flight from Los Angeles to New York City. The Lindbergh Line was a luxury airline. Passengers sat in wicker seats, and plane windows had brown velvet curtains. Each seat had an electric cigar lighter and ashtray (smoking was allowed on planes then). Passengers could watch newsreels and cartoons on TAT, the first "in-flight movies." They were also given a solid gold fountain pen as a souvenir of their flight.

AHEAD OF ITS TIME

The airline could cross the country in 48 hours, beating railroad times by 24 hours. But the ticket price was expensive, and too few businessmen were willing to pay for the reduction in travel time. TAT lost around $3 million and ended service after about a year and a half. It proved to be an airline that was ahead of its time. ☀

GOGGLES PROTECT AGAINST WIND IN OPEN COCKPIT

Charles Lindbergh

TAT planes offered a more comfortable ride than any other airline at the time.

BIRTH OF THE JET AIRPLANE

With the coming of World War II (1939–1945), airplanes took another giant step forward. The United States needed warplanes to fight its enemies. President Franklin D. Roosevelt called for the plane industry to increase production, going from 6,000 planes a year to a minimum of 50,000. By 1944, U.S. aircraft manufacturers were producing about 100,000 planes a year.

These planes were designed to fly farther and with more power than any previous airplane. Airports were built across the country and around the world to accommodate these long-distance fliers, making flying boats obsolete. Other technological developments improved air flight. Radar allowed pilots to navigate at night or in bad weather. Radio communications with ground stations were greatly improved. Most important of all was the development of the turbojet engine. This high-speed engine allowed jet planes to reach speeds and distances never achieved before.

B-24 Liberator bomber planes lined up in an American factory during World War II

Flight attendants provided food, beverages, and anything else passengers needed during flights.

THE GOLDEN AGE OF AIR TRAVEL

When the war ended, many American warplanes were turned into commercial airplanes. Jet planes such as the Douglas DC-8 and Boeing 707 were able to hold more than 150 passengers and fly at speeds greater than 500 miles per hour (805 kph). Average airfares began to drop in the years following the war, allowing middle-class Americans to fly for the first time to exotic places for dream vacations. Businessmen came to rely on jet travel to attend conferences and meetings with distant clients. Major airlines such as Pan Am and Trans World Airlines (TWA) dominated the market for overseas flights. Domestic flights were operated mainly by the airlines American, Delta, and United. In 1984, United became the first airline to provide service to all 50 states.

Airlines tried to make traveling to a destination as much fun as arriving there. Female airline attendants, then called stewardesses, provided passengers with everything from beverages and hot meals to pillows and blankets for overnight flights.

The first hub airports could become very crowded during peak flying times.

DEREGULATION

Under regulations enforced by the Civil Aeronautics Board (CAB), airfares were carefully controlled. Airlines could not try to compete with each other by lowering prices. In 1978, Congress passed the Airline **Deregulation** Act. The new law gradually phased out the CAB and removed government controls over airline fares, routes, and the entry of new airlines into the marketplace. The Federal Aviation Administration (FAA) continued, however, to oversee safety regulations on all commercial airlines.

Deregulation allowed airlines the freedom to compete. This started a fare war, with each airline trying to undercut the others. Airlines established hubs in an effort to become more efficient and keep airfares down. Hubs were large, central airports where most flights connected. From hubs, smaller flights continued to other destinations. While the hub system made flying more efficient, it also clogged airports and airways and reduced the number of nonstop flights.

THE RISE OF THE REGIONAL AIRLINE

Deregulation led to the birth of many smaller, regional airlines, such as People Express, which began operating in 1981. People Express slashed in-flight services to lower fares for the budget-conscious traveler. This helped it become extremely popular. Other new airlines, such as New York Air, specialized in shuttle services between three major cities—Washington, D.C., New York, and Boston. Other existing regional airlines, such as Frontier, expanded nationally. These innovative airlines made use of small jets powered by highly efficient turbofan jet engines. Before long, budget airlines began to seriously cut into the business of the major airlines.

MOVABLE STAIRCASE FOR OUTDOOR BOARDING

Passengers board a People Express plane in 1985.

A prototype of the Concorde jet is moved out of a hangar in France in 1968.

THE CONCORDE

By the early 1960s, the expense of developing new aircraft was so high that countries were pooling their resources. In November 1962, Great Britain and France went to work on the first commercial jet that would travel faster than the speed of sound. This **supersonic** plane was called the Concorde.

BUILT FOR SPEED

Seven years in the making, the Concorde had its first test flight in 1969. Its sleek body was streamlined for high speeds. It had "delta wings," which were small, triangle-shaped wings that rode over the air smoothly. The Concorde's most distinctive feature was its long, pointed nose. The nose could be raised for flight and lowered for takeoffs and landings to give pilots a better view of the runway.

A Concorde jet lowers its nose to prepare for takeoff.

A CONTROVERSIAL PLANE

The first Concorde passenger flight took place on January 21, 1976. It could fly from London to New York City in four hours, nearly half the time it took a traditional jet like the Boeing 747 to make the same trip. The cost of a round-trip ticket on the Concorde was originally $9,000, which put it out of reach to anyone who wasn't wealthy.

There was also a more serious draw-back to the world's fastest commercial plane. Breaking the sound barrier created a sonic boom that followed the Concorde wherever it flew. The noise was deafening and, many argued, harmful to the environment.

Firefighters deal with the wreckage of the 2000 Concorde crash in France.

The United States worked on developing its own supersonic transport (SST) but abandoned the project in 1971. As for the Concorde, a fatal crash in 2000 in France added to its troubles, and the plane made its final flight in November 2003. 💥

Take off...

CONCORDE INAUGURAL FLIGHT 21st JANUARY 1976

TROUBLING TIMES

By the early 1980s, airlines both large and small were facing big troubles. Many had overexpanded their operations and suddenly found themselves ill-equipped to deal with a shrinking market. A world shortage of oil made fuel prices soar. Worker strikes, such as the air traffic controllers strike in 1981, added to the trouble. Economic troubles further hurt business. Poorly managed airlines such as Eastern and Braniff went bankrupt and closed. So did small airlines such as People Express. Pan Am, once a giant in the airline industry, was forced to sell off many of its assets. However, major airlines such as American, United, and Delta survived the troubles through careful management.

Eastern Airlines was one of many aviation companies that had financial problems in the 1980s.

The destruction of Pan Am flight 103 made headlines around the world.

CRIME IN THE SKIES

Another challenge the airline industry faced was crime. **Hijacking** of commercial airplanes in flight had been a problem since at least the 1960s. Hijackers would commandeer a plane and force the pilot to alter its route and fly to another destination. Once the plane landed somewhere that was safe for the hijackers, the passengers and crew might be released or held for ransom. The FAA responded with increased security measures in the 1970s. It introduced armed sky marshals on flights. It also added metal detectors and x-ray screenings for boarding passengers and luggage at airports.

Plane piracy entered a new era in the 1980s as terrorists began hijacking airplanes or planting bombs on them. One of these incidents resulted in the explosion of Pan Am flight 103 over Lockerbie, Scotland, in 1988. All 258 people aboard died. The disaster contributed to Pan Am going out of business three years later.

But the worst was yet to come. On a beautiful Monday morning in September 2001, a tragedy occurred that changed the American air travel industry forever.

Air travel has become an important part of everyday life for many people.

2

AIR TRAVEL TODAY

Air travel has changed greatly in the 21st century. Computers and the Internet have saved passengers time and effort in planning their flights and getting tickets and boarding passes. On the other hand, heightened airport security has added time to the flying experience and made it more difficult. Lower fares have drawn many people to air travel, but the services they once took for granted have vanished or been saddled with extra costs. While air travel is no longer in a golden age, it has remained an important part of our lives and will continue to be so.

LANDMARK AIRPORTS

1909	1928	1963	2009
Aviator Wilbur Wright opens Maryland's College Park Airport, the world's oldest continuously operating airport.	The future Los Angeles International Airport is born on 640 acres of a former ranch.	New York's Idlewild Airport is renamed JFK International Airport in honor of the 35th president. Today, it is the country's largest international gateway airport.	Branson Airport, the only privately owned and operated commercial airport in the United States, opens in Missouri.

GLOVES PROTECT WORKERS FROM GERMS OR HARMFUL SUBSTANCES IN LUGGAGE

TRAVELERS LOAD PERSONAL ITEMS INTO PLASTIC BINS FOR INSPECTION

Security workers check passengers' luggage for dangerous or illegal objects.

9/11 AND NEW SECURITY MEASURES

On the morning of September 11, 2001, terrorists hijacked four commercial airplanes. They crashed two of the planes into the World Trade Center towers in New York City. Another one was piloted into the Pentagon near Washington, D.C. Passengers fought the terrorists on the fourth plane, causing it to crash in a Pennsylvania field. Nearly 3,000 people died, in the airplanes and in the struck buildings combined. Commercial air travel was suspended entirely for days.

Authorities in government and the airline business created stronger security measures to prevent another such tragedy. The Transportation Security Adminstration (TSA) was established by Congress in November 2001 to take control of airline security. Federal workers were hired to handle all passenger and baggage inspection. Ultimately, passengers not only had to go through x-ray screenings but also were required to take off belts and shoes for inspection. They could no longer bring containers holding more than 3.4 ounces (100 ml) of liquids, gels, or creams on flights. Despite these preventive measures, the fear of terrorism in the skies combined with a slowing economy caused a decline in air travel for several years.

AIR SAFETY

Despite people's fears of terrorism and accidents, air travel remains the safest form of transportation today. More people die in automobile accidents every three months than have died in the entire history of commercial aviation. The safety of air travel is a result not only of tightened security but also of improved technology and organization. Computerized instruments help pilots get through rough situations in the air. Air traffic controllers and their sophisticated computer screens keep plane traffic flowing smoothly and safely. Oxygen masks and flotation devices help passengers in the rare event of a flight emergency. Evacuation slides and rafts help get them off a plane in a crash on land or in water. The FAA Safety Team (FAAST) runs educational courses and seminars on air safety for airline employees. The Aviation Safety Action Program encourages employees to voluntarily report the airline safety issues they discover.

Flight attendants show passengers how to operate the safety equipment aboard the plane before every flight.

PULLING STRINGS CAUSES
LIFE VEST TO INFLATE

FROM THIS TO THAT

AIRPORT SCANNERS

Many airports use x-ray scanners at boarding checkpoints to examine passengers' clothing and bodies for weapons or bombs. This type of scanner became a part of standard security procedures in 2008. These backscatter scanners give security personnel a detailed image of a person's anatomy, highlighting any irregular shapes under clothing.

Passengers must raise their arms as they are scanned in order to give security workers a clear view of their bodies.

A CONTROVERSIAL ISSUE

Backscatter scanners were not a popular addition to airports. Many people protested that the scanners were an invasion of privacy. They called for the scanner to be banned. There was also the possibility of the x-rays being harmful to health. Finally, the scanners did not work perfectly. Buttons and folds in clothing were sometimes wrongly read as suspicious objects. The FAA agreed with the criticism and began working to replace the scanners with ones that were less invasive.

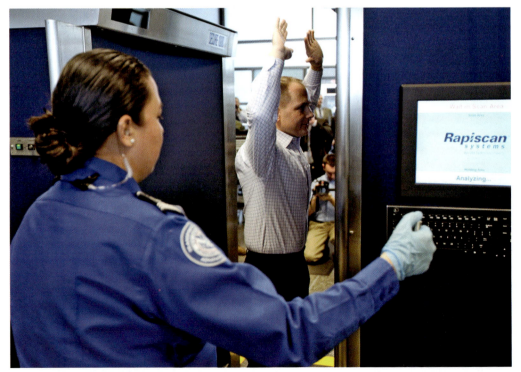

YELLOW BOXES INDICATE PLACES WHERE PEOPLE MIGHT BE CARRYING CONCEALED OBJECTS

Newer scanners are just as effective, but less invasive to passengers' privacy.

A NEW KIND OF SCANNER

In May 2013, Advanced Imaging Technology (AIT) replaced the original scanners with ones that only give a general outline of the passenger's body. Anything suspicious under clothing pops up as a small, yellow box on the screen. Because the images are less graphic, security officers can view them openly in public areas and not in remote rooms as was done earlier, making the procedure more efficient. The new scanners use the same kind of radio waves sent out by cell phones. They are less likely to cause health issues than x-rays. ✹

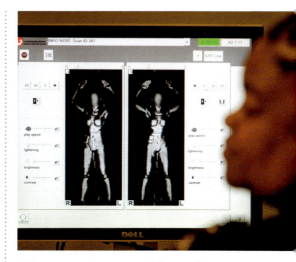

Older scanners were criticized for revealing too much about passengers' bodies.

BIGGER AND BETTER

As new designs and better technology were developed, transport planes became bigger and better. For years, the standard for large, luxurious aircraft was the Boeing 747. Known as the jumbo jet, it can hold about 500 passengers and is still used often today.

The wide-body plane entered a new era with the emergence of the Airbus, developed as a joint effort by France, Germany, Spain, and the United Kingdom. Airbus's A300 model, first flown in 1974, was the world's first twin-engine wide-body jet. Over the years, Airbus continued to design new and often bigger aircraft. In 2007, it launched the A380, a double-deck, wide-body, four-engine jet that seats 525 passengers in one **configuration**. Up to 853 people can fit if the plane is arranged in an all-economy-class configuration. This plane is so big that some airports had to expand their hangars to accommodate it.

The Airbus A380 is one of the largest passenger jets in history.

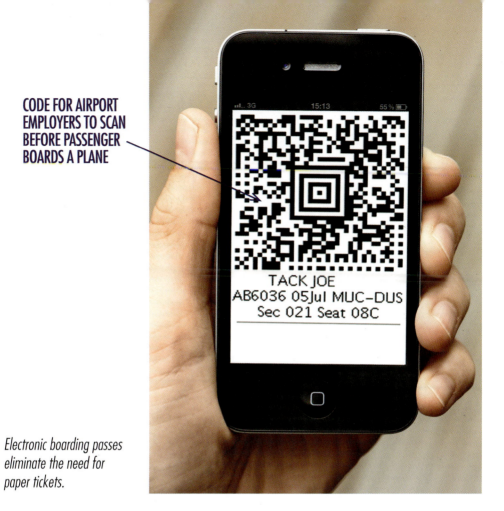

CODE FOR AIRPORT EMPLOYERS TO SCAN BEFORE PASSENGER BOARDS A PLANE

Electronic boarding passes eliminate the need for paper tickets.

FLYING IN THE COMPUTER AGE

Just as commercial planes have become bigger and better, so have the services provided to air travelers. In the past, travelers had to call airlines on the telephone to make a reservation. Thanks to the spread of Internet service and mobile devices, travelers can now book flights from almost anywhere. Ticket buyers can even download boarding passes to their devices and avoid long lines at the airport. They can also check online for flight delays or any other updates. Nearly all airports offer wireless service, so passengers can access the Internet while waiting for flights. Wireless Internet access is even available midair on most flights, though there is usually a charge for this service.

MODERN MARVEL

Modern airports often look a lot like shopping malls.

AIRPORTS BIG AND SMALL

Once little more than small areas with runways where planes took off and landed, airports have become vast complexes for air travel. They can accommodate millions of passengers and thousands of flights every year. The largest airports are like small cities. They include not only airline booths and waiting areas, but also shops, restaurants, and even nightclubs.

KING OF AMERICAN AIRPORTS

No modern American airport is as impressive as the Hartsfield-Jackson Atlanta International Airport, the busiest in the country. Established in 1925 on an abandoned auto racetrack, the Georgia airport grew steadily over the years. In

An aerial view of Hartsfield-Jackson Atlanta International Airport

The massive atrium is one of the most recent additions to Hartsfield-Jackson.

1980, the airport was expanded and renamed in honor of former mayor William Hartsfield. (Mayor Maynard Jackson's name was added in 2003.) It was 2.5 million square feet (232,000 square meters) in size and could handle more than 55 million passengers and 16 airlines.

BIGGER AND BIGGER

More improvements have been added since then, including the 1.3 million-square-foot (120,000 sq m) International **Concourse**, which is the largest international facility in the country. Less than two years later, a three-story **atrium** was built. Over the past decade, the airport has won numerous awards from magazines and organizations for being the best large U.S. airport, the world's most efficient airport, and the top American airport for Wi-Fi connectivity. More recent additions include a recycling program and a dog park. ☀

Emirates Airlines offers luxurious accommodations to its passengers.

NO GOLDEN AGE

While deregulation opened up air travel to competition and gave potential travelers more value for their money, there has been a long-term downside. Few major airlines survived the post-deregulation competition. This has lowered competition among the remaining airlines. Expenses in fuel costs and other resources have raised ticket prices again.

If there is growth in the air travel industry, it comes from the small percentage of travelers who can afford first class. Foreign airlines such as Emirates Airlines offer private compartments with flat-screen television and luxury bathrooms on some long-distance flights. Other airlines offer free limo service to and from the airport for first-class customers. Delta has recently converted its frequent flyer miles to frequent flyer dollars. Customers earn points based not on how far they fly, but on how much money they spend.

CRAMPED IN COACH

The majority of passengers who fly coach feel they are paying more for air travel and getting less for it. Meals have been eliminated on many domestic flights and cost extra on some longer flights. There is often a fee for any luggage beyond one small bag. The number of seats on many planes has been increased, leaving less room for passengers to stretch their legs.

There is even a decline in airports. In a Skytrax survey ranking global airports based on customer satisfaction, no American airport placed in the top 25. Only four made the top 50. The American public seems less happy with air travel than ever before. It will take good marketing, original ideas, and an improvement in airplanes and airports to win back the American consumer. At one time or another, many of us will find ourselves needing to fly, and hopefully the experience will be a positive one. It has been so in the past, and it can be again in the future.

On most modern flights, seats are close together and services such as food cost extra.

VIDEO SCREENS DISPLAY IN-FLIGHT ENTERTAINMENT AND INSTRUCTIONAL VIDEOS

TRAYS FOLD DOWN FROM SEATS TO SAVE SPACE

Pilots and other airline and airport employees work together to provide safe, reliable travel to passengers.

3

CAREERS IN AIR TRAVEL

I t takes many skilled professionals to put an airplane and its passengers in the air and get them down again safely. Each person has a job to do. The pilot steers the plane. The flight attendant sees to the needs of each passenger. The ground crew maintains the plane. The air traffic controller helps guide the plane to its destination. All of these people work together as a team. Each airline relies on its staff and crew to make flights safe, efficient, and pleasant whether traveling between two neighboring cities or across the globe.

ATTENDING TO THE PASSENGERS

1929	1930	1942	1971
Transcontinental Air Transport (TAT) hires some of the first flight stewards; they are all young men.	Boeing Air Transport hires Ellen Church, a registered nurse, as the first airline stewardess.	As nurses go off to serve in World War II, airlines begin hiring non-nurses as stewardesses.	A federal court rules that men may not be discriminated against in the hiring process for flight attendants (the term that replaced stewardesses).

The inside of a flight simulator is an exact copy of a real plane's cockpit.

EDUCATION AND TRAINING

Some education and specific training beyond high school are essential for most careers in the air travel industry. Pilots and copilots must attend a private flight school or be accepted into an airline's training program. Some learn to fly as part of their military service. Candidates for airline pilot jobs must be at least 23 years old and have a commercial pilot's license with 1,500 hours of flight time.

Flight attendants with some college education have a better chance of finding a job than those with only a high school diploma. Newly hired attendants must take a three- to seven-week course run by the airline. It includes classroom work and in-flight experience in a simulated airplane cabin.

Technical workers such as aviation mechanics and computer specialists need to take courses at technical schools. Highly skilled workers such as aeronautical engineers need a college degree.

THE CAPTAIN OF THE SHIP

There are usually two pilots on a commercial airline flight. The senior pilot is the captain. The copilot is the first officer. On rare flights using older planes, there might be a flight engineer along who monitors the instruments and the plane's engines. Besides being responsible for the steering and navigating of the plane, the captain prepares a detailed flight plan before each flight. The captain will also speak to the crew and passengers, pointing out important landmarks they are flying over, reporting updated arrival times, and warning of **turbulence** and other inconveniences they may experience. In a crisis, the pilot must maintain control of the plane and, in emergency situations, try to land safely.

Until quite recently, airline pilots were exclusively men. In 1973, American Airlines became the first major airline to hire a female pilot. In 2011, there were about 8,175 female commercial pilots, a small percentage of the total number. Only 450 of these women were captains.

There are at least two pilots on any commercial flight.

AN INTERVIEW WITH AERONAUTICAL ENGINEER JACOB ZEIGER

Jacob Zeiger is a production support engineer for Boeing, the world's largest aerospace company and leading manufacturer of commercial jetliners and military aircraft. In his job, he troubleshoots problems with new airplanes and makes structural repairs when necessary before the planes are delivered to an airline. He also serves as a field service representative for Boeing, meeting with airlines at their home offices to help them keep their fleets flying.

When did you first realize that you wanted to be an aeronautical engineer? Did any person or event inspire that career choice? When I was four years old, an uncle took me to an air show where I saw the Blue Angels, the U.S. Navy flight demonstration squadron, perform. I was completely amazed by these aircraft and the men who flew them. Even the crisp way they walked to their aircraft impressed me. I'm still in awe to this day of how pilots work together in perfect harmony to perform in an air show or on a flight. I was hooked on planes. Then when I was 13, during a visit to my grandmother in Omaha, Nebraska, I asked my parents to drop me off at the airport for the day. I spent the entire day checking out every part of the airport and talking to everyone from the air traffic controller to the pilot who would fly the airplane. I told everyone I was writing a report for school. I just wanted to learn everything I could about airplanes and how they worked.

What kinds of classes did you take in high school and college that prepared you for your career? I took lots of science and advanced math courses in high school to prepare me for engineering school. I attended what is now the Missouri University of Science and Technology, where I took more physics courses, lots of math courses, and classes in aerodynamics and plane structure.

What was your first job like? At 16, still in high school, I began flying lessons at my local airport. The airport owner liked me, and soon I was working for him on weekends, holidays, and over summer vacation. I worked on repairing airplanes as his apprentice and ran the airport on weekends when the owner was away. Then in college I worked as a dispatcher for a local airline, Baron Aviation, that transports cargo. These early jobs were important because they taught me the language of aviation, something you don't learn in engineering school. It made me more valuable when I got the job at Boeing.

What projects have you worked on that you're especially proud of? Boeing recently developed a new version of the 747, the 747-8. I got to help build the very first of these airplanes, participated in its 18-month flight test program, and was even present to help the first airlines start operating it. The experience let me see how airplanes are built and operated from every angle.

It takes a team of people to produce and work on an airplane. Does working as part of a team come naturally to you? There are two parts to my answer to this question. On one hand, I have always found it natural to be part of a team. But, on the other hand, learning how to communicate with other members of the teams I've been on at Boeing has been a learning experience. It has taken time to know the right person to go to with questions and information.

Let's say someone gave you whatever you needed to design and build your dream airplane. What would it look like and what would it do? My dream airplane is one that is easy to fly and maintain and is made with components that don't break down very often. It would have a simple design. I find that complexity in design can lead to failure in aviation.

What advice would you give to a young person who wants to work in aeronautics one day? I would tell them to make it obvious to everyone around them what it is they want to do—today, next year, and 10 years from now. They should share with everyone around them whatever it is that they're enthusiastic about. Other people will help to keep that passion alive. ☀

FLIGHT ATTENDANTS

The flight attendant is the face of the air travel industry for most passengers. Flight attendants have many jobs to perform. They greet passengers, make sure they're comfortable, and answer any questions they have about the flight. They serve beverages, snacks, and meals and provide earphones for listening to music or movies. More importantly, they see that passengers are safe and that they follow instructions. Attendants are also trained to provide first aid in case of physical accidents or other health problems. They must have excellent people skills to help reassure a child traveling alone or calm down an upset adult passenger. A good flight attendant genuinely likes people and is eager to make every flight enjoyable. However, the attendant's number one priority is always to be ready to secure or evacuate the plane in the event of an emergency.

Flight attendants show passengers how to fasten their safety belts correctly.

Engineers make sure that every part of an airplane is working properly.

BEHIND THE SCENES

Most passengers never see maintenance engineers, air traffic controllers, aeronautical engineers, computer specialists, or mechanics. However, these workers are all crucial to a smooth and safe flight. Maintenance engineers are responsible for checking out the plane before takeoff to make sure everything is in working order. If anything is wrong, their crew of mechanics will fix or repair it.

Air traffic controllers work from screens inside the airport. They have the demanding job of making sure the flow of air traffic is safe and orderly. They use radio and radar to stay in contact with pilots as they prepare for takeoff or landing. When there is bad weather, a frequent problem in air travel, they try to minimize the problem by rerouting air traffic.

Baggage handlers load and unload passenger luggage as well as other cargo on the plane. They must work quickly and efficiently to make sure passengers can pick up their luggage in the airport in a timely manner after leaving the plane.

THE ARTISTIC SIDE

Continental Airlines planes were known for their distinctive tail art.

COLOR AND DESIGN

Although air travel may appear more technological than creative, artists, designers, and writers all contribute to making air travel exciting. Artists and designers come up with color schemes and designs to make the interiors and exteriors of planes appealing to passengers. Southwest Airlines has a heart painted on the side entry door of every one of its planes. This warm symbol represents the company's headquarters at Love Field, a Texas airport. Continental Airlines, a victim of the deregulation era, painted planes' tails gold and called itself "the proud bird with the golden tail." Pacific

Southwest Airlines, which served the state of California from 1949 to 1988, had an artist paint a smile under the **cockpit** at the front of its planes. The smile went with the company's slogan, "Catch Our Smile."

FINE ART ON DISPLAY

Airports buy fine art such as paintings and sculptures to decorate their atriums and hallways. Famous artists including Frank Stella and Roy Lichtenstein have sold their works to airports. Some airports are even home to art museums with changing exhibits. One of the most art-conscious airports is San Francisco International. It has spent more than $15 million on

San Francisco International Airport is known for its extensive collection of artwork.

art since the 1970s. As one writer puts it, "If you want to see some of the best contemporary art in American cities these days, buy an airline ticket."

READ ALL ABOUT IT

Catchy slogans and ad copy are another way that airlines get customers' attention. Writers on marketing teams come up with the text. Perhaps the most successful slogan in air travel history is United's "Fly the Friendly Skies." Most airlines also publish a monthly or bimonthly magazine that employs editors, writers, photographers, and illustrators. These magazines are placed in the forward pouch of each passenger's seat. They contain articles on travel, food, entertainment, and other topics for passengers to read on flights and take with them when they leave the plane. ☀

In-flight magazines provide entertainment and information to travelers.

Flight instructors teach pilots the skills they need to fly safely.

SUPPORT SYSTEMS

There are many skilled professionals in air travel who serve and support other employees. Flight and ground instructors help pilots and copilots learn the latest systems in new aircraft. Flight instructors help in the air, and ground instructors assist with operations before takeoff. These workers are often retired pilots. Other instructors are employees of airplane manufacturers. They provide heavy support to airlines so that their airplanes are always in the safest possible configuration.

Aviation doctors give physicals and regular health checks to pilots and other employees, making sure that they are up to the demands of their jobs. Airline pursers manage money needed to purchase supplies, food, and other items necessary for flights. They also oversee the work of flight attendants.

AIRPORT WORKERS

Airports are like small cities that care for passengers and crew alike as they wait to board or get off their flights. Millions of people from all around the world cross paths at these travel hubs. Airports have their own employees to keep these travelers safe and happy. Airport security guards and agents watch out for crime and inspect passengers and their luggage as they enter boarding areas. Skycaps help people get their luggage to the ticket line. Finally, there are the employees who work in the many shops, restaurants, and other businesses that are the lifeblood of any large airport.

Customer service employees at airports take tickets and answer any questions passengers might have.

An airplane takes off from
LaGuardia Airport in New York City.

4

FROM TAKEOFF TO LANDING

A commercial airplane flight, whether domestic or international, is made up of many steps. Most of these procedures are unseen by the passengers, who take their journeys for granted. But the pilots, attendants, ground crews, air traffic controllers, and other workers on and off the plane must perform each step carefully to ensure that the flight will be a safe and pleasant one and that the plane will arrive on time at its destination. Let's follow one domestic flight from its preparation to takeoff to landing and see what happens at each step along the way.

LEGENDARY AIRLINES

1920	1928	1930	1953
Royal Dutch Airlines, the world's oldest operating airline, begins flights.	Delta Air Lines is founded.	Trans World Airlines begins offering the first transcontinental flights.	British Overseas Airways begins the first regularly scheduled jet airplane flights.

A ground crew member cleans the windshield of a cockpit as part of the preflight preparation process.

PREP TIME

The flight crew arrives at the airport about an hour before takeoff. The captain and first officer check into the pilot's lounge, and the captain gets the flight data from a computer. These data include the weather, number of passengers, and names of the other crew members. Using this information, the captain works out a flight plan detailing the plane's speed and altitude, the amount of fuel needed, and the weather patterns along the travel route. That information is then given to the air traffic controller.

Around the same time, a maintenance technician checks the airplane's systems to ensure there are no problems that would prevent a safe flight. The technician also performs routine maintenance as needed.

Once the airplane has arrived at the gate, the flight attendants and pilots meet to go over the flight schedule. The first officer makes a general inspection of the plane to see that all is in order for takeoff. Then the first officer and the captain go to the cockpit to check out the instruments.

ALL ABOARD

The lead attendant assigns each flight attendant to a section of the cabin that he or she will be responsible for. There is one attendant for every 50 passengers on a flight. Once the attendants have their spots, it's time for the passengers to board the airplane. The attendants greet them with a smile and direct them to their seats. They help passengers stow their carry-on luggage in the overhead compartments and small bags under their seats. Once the passengers are settled in, the attendants review safety procedures or play a prerecorded safety video.

While this is going on, the pilots are preparing for takeoff. The captain signs a flight release and receives the latest weather information, passenger count, and predeparture clearance from the control tower and gate agents.

Bags must be safely stowed away before a flight so they do not fall down and hurt anyone as the plane takes off.

WHERE THE MAGIC HAPPENS

THE FEDERAL AVIATION ADMINISTRATION

Founded in 1958, the Federal Aviation Administration (FAA) is the agency of the U.S. Department of Transportation that controls air traffic. It also creates and enforces air safety regulations and air traffic procedures. Finally, it certifies airplanes, airports, pilots, and other airline personnel. After the terrible events of September 11, 2001, it was the FAA that designed procedures for antiterrorist security in all American airports.

FAA administrator Michael Huerta

RESEARCH AND DEVELOPMENT

The FAA is more than a lawmaker and enforcer. It supports cutting-edge research that will help develop new ways to improve air traffic, aerospace systems, and airway facilities. One ambitious project the FAA is currently working on is called NextGen. The NextGen program is redesigning airspace to make it safer and to manage flights in it more efficiently.

Students listen to the manager of an aircraft maintenance facility during an Aviation Career Education Academy event.

EDUCATION OUTREACH

The FAA also works to foster interest in aviation and aerospace in young people. Every summer it runs Aviation Career Education (ACE) Academies. These summer camps are aimed at middle school and high school students interested in aviation. At ACE Academies, students can experience flying by way of a flight simulator, take field trips to aviation sites such as museums and air shows, and even try flying a real plane. The organization also sponsors Adopt-A-School projects, where it provides funds and expertise to schools so they can better teach students science, technology, and math. The FAA does all this to meet its central mission "to provide the safest, most efficient aerospace system in the world."

READY FOR TAKEOFF

The attendants perform a final check of the entire cabin. They check that each passenger's seat belt is secured and that each seat is in the upright position. Then an attendant secures the plane's door. Next, the captain lets the ground crew members know that they can move the plane away from the gate and onto the runway. The pilots wait to receive word from the air traffic controller that they are next in line for takeoff. Then they tell the attendants to prepare for takeoff and strap themselves into their jump seats.

There are no unnecessary activities or conversations in the cockpit until the plane reaches 10,000 feet (3,048 m) and a speed of 270 to 350 **knots**. Then the flight settles into cruising mode. The captain signals the attendants with a chime that they can now get out of their seats and begin serving passengers. The cockpit crew can attend to record keeping, monitoring instruments, or other administrative duties.

COMPUTERS SHOW FLIGHT PATHS OF AIRPLANES IN THE SKY

Air traffic controllers ensure that planes do not crash into each other in midair.

Flight attendants provide many services to passengers, but their main concern is safety.

PASSENGER SERVICE

As the plane continues to climb, the attendants prepare and load the beverage trolley and begin serving the passengers. They may also distribute earphones so passengers can listen to music channels or watch TV programs or an in-flight movie on overhead or seatback monitors. Around this time, the captain will usually make an announcement about flight time to the destination, describe weather conditions on the route, or refer to points of interest the plane will pass over. If conditions permit, the passengers might be allowed to move around the cabin and use the restroom. If there is turbulence or some other difficulty in the air, the "fasten seat belt" sign will come on. Passengers will be required to return to their seats and buckle up.

LASTING CONTRIBUTIONS

BLACK BOXES

Though plane crashes are rare, aircraft manufacturers and airlines must still plan for the worst. When a plane crashes and there are no survivors, there is often only one way for investigators to find out what happened. They must recover the plane's "black box." The black box is misnamed. It is not black but instead is usually a bright orange or yellow to make it easier to see in a plane's wreckage. It is also not one box but two. They are the Cockpit Voice Recorder (CVR) and the Flight Data Recorder (FDR). These two devices are located in the tail of a plane, where they are least likely to be damaged in a crash.

A Cockpit Voice Recorder

WHAT THEY DO

The CVR monitors voices and sounds in the cockpit. Trained experts can evaluate every ping and hum of the engine to help determine what went wrong. The crew's conversation before the crash may provide more clues. The FDR records multiple operations of the plane all at once, such as the time, the plane's altitude, the direction of the flight, and much more. By reading these data, investigators can often determine what caused the crash. They can also use the data to create a computer video reconstruction of the flight.

A Flight Data Recorder

Experts were unable to determine the cause of the crash of a Comet jet in Italy in 1954.

FIFTY-YEAR HISTORY

The black box was invented by an Australian scientist named David Warren. Warren was inspired by the unexplained crash of the first jet-powered commercial plane in 1954. He demonstrated the first black box in 1957. Within three years, it was mandatory equipment on all Australian commercial aircraft. Over the years, the black box has become more sophisticated. However, its basic function has changed little. People hope a plane's black box will never need to be used, but when a tragedy occurs it is indispensable in determining what caused a plane to crash. Engineers and airline officials can use this information to prevent similar crashes from happening in the future. This is one of the many reasons air travel has become so safe in modern times. ☀

An FDR is stored in the tail of a plane.

Weather conditions can affect the way pilots land a plane.

PREPARE TO LAND

When there are about 30 to 40 minutes remaining in the flight, the captain will begin the plane's descent. One pilot radios the destination airport to give them the estimated time of touchdown and make any special requests for passengers needing wheelchairs or connecting flights. In turn, the airport sends any restrictions for approach and landing and gives current weather conditions on the ground. When the plane descends to about 10,000 feet (3,048 m), the captain alerts the cabin crew to make final landing preparations. This includes making sure all passengers are wearing their seat belts and that all areas in the cabin are secure and clean.

BACK ON THE GROUND

To make the landing as smooth as possible, the pilots use reverse thrust and wheel brakes as the plane touches down on the runway. The first officer contacts ground control for instructions on where to go and confirms the arrival gate assignment. If the gate is currently occupied by another plane, the captain will **taxi** to another location until the gate is free.

When the plane is at its arrival gate, the pilot shuts down the engines and the ground crew moves the **jet bridge** into position at the exit doors. The seat belt sign is turned off, and attendants help passengers leave the plane. Wheelchair passengers and unaccompanied children are usually helped off last. The flight crew is the last to leave the plane after a final check of the facilities. Crew members continuing on with the flight begin to prepare for the next leg of the journey. If another crew is taking over for a new flight, the current crew will usually meet with them. If it is the last flight of the day for the airplane, the crew is released from duty. It has been another safe and successful flight, and there are many more to come.

Jet bridges connect planes to airport terminals.

THE FUTURE

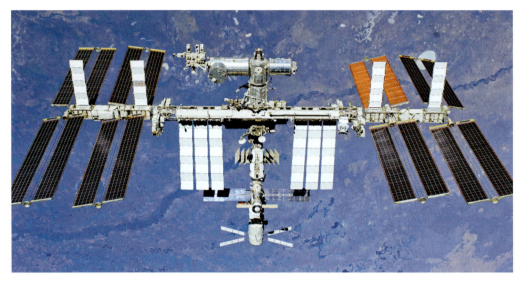

In recent years, some people have been able to visit the International Space Station.

SPACE TOURISM

The next challenge for air travel may be literally out of this world. Several commercial airlines are preparing to take passengers into outer space, a place where only astronauts and trained scientists had gone before.

RUSSIA TAKES THE LEAD

The only carrier to date that has taken paying passengers into space is the Russian Federal Space Agency. From 2001 to 2010, it took private citizens on board the *Soyuz* spacecraft to the *International Space Station (ISS)*, where astronauts from several countries live and work. The cost of a ticket into space ranged from $20 million to $40 million. Russia stopped the service in 2010 because space was needed on the ships for an increased number of ISS crew members.

Meanwhile, the American company SpaceX, founded in 2002, has been delivering payloads to the *ISS* since May 2012. SpaceX says that its ultimate goal is to enable people from Earth to travel to and live on other planets.

Richard Branson dreams of making it easy for anyone to visit space.

TO THE MOON AND BEYOND

Perhaps the leading airline to chart a course for space tourism is Great Britain's Virgin Galactic, a spin-off of Virgin Atlantic Airways. Its owner, Richard Branson, promised that he and his children would be the first passengers on Virgin's maiden voyage into space in late 2014. Skeptics argue that Virgin hasn't yet mastered the technology to send its *SpaceShipTwo* safely into space.

But hundreds of people, including many celebrities, have already paid to be among Branson's first customers for a two-hour flight into space, with five minutes of weightlessness. The price? At least $250,000.

SpaceX's Dragon is an unmanned spacecraft that transports supplies to the ISS from Earth.

Branson is also thinking about high-speed point-to-point flights on Earth. His *SpaceShipTwo* could possibly take passengers from London to Los Angeles in about two hours. He has even talked about flying people around the moon by 2043. When it comes to air travel, the sky might not be the limit! ☀

Virgin Galactic's SpaceShipTwo

CAREER STATS

AIRLINE AND COMMERCIAL PILOTS

MEDIAN ANNUAL SALARY (2012): $98,410

NUMBER OF JOBS (2012): 104,100

PROJECTED JOB GROWTH: −1%, little or no change

PROJECTED CHANGE IN JOBS: −800

REQUIRED EDUCATION: Bachelor's degree

LICENSE/CERTIFICATION: Commercial pilot's license from the FAA, Airline Transport Pilot (ATP) certificate

FLIGHT ATTENDANTS

MEDIAN ANNUAL SALARY (2012): $37,240

NUMBER OF JOBS (2012): 84,800

PROJECTED JOB GROWTH: −7%, a decline

PROJECTED CHANGE IN JOBS (2012): −5,500

REQUIRED EDUCATION: High school diploma or equivalent required, some college preferred

LICENSE/CERTIFICATION: Certification program provided by airline

AIR TRAFFIC CONTROLLERS

MEDIAN ANNUAL SALARY (2012): $122,530

NUMBER OF JOBS (2012): 25,000

PROJECTED JOB GROWTH: 1%, little or no change

PROJECTED CHANGE IN JOBS (2012): 400

REQUIRED EDUCATION: Associate's degree

LICENSE/CERTIFICATION: FAA Academy training course certificate

Figures reported by the United States Bureau of Labor Statistics

RESOURCES

BOOKS

Nahum, Andrew. *Flight*. New York: DK Children's, 2011.

Williams, Jasmine. *All About Airplanes: A Picture Book for Kids About Airplanes*. Twilight Publishing, 2013.

FACTS FOR NOW

Visit this Scholastic Web site for more information on air travel:
www.factsfornow.scholastic.com
Enter the keywords **Air Travel**

GLOSSARY

altitudes (AL-ti-toodz) heights of something above the ground or above sea level

atrium (AY-tree-uhm) an open area inside a building

cabins (KAB-inz) sections of an airplane for the passengers, crew, or cargo

cockpit (KAHK-pit) the control area in the front of a plane, boat, or spacecraft where the pilot and sometimes the crew sit

concourse (KAHN-kors) a large open space or thoroughfare for people in an airport

configuration (kuhn-fig-yuh-RAY-shun) the arrangement of the parts or components of a thing

deregulation (dee-reg-yuh-LAY-shun) the reduction of government control over an industry

gondola (GAHN-duh-luh) a cabin or enclosure for passengers under a hot-air balloon or blimp

hijacking (HYE-jak-ing) taking illegal control of a vehicle and forcing its pilot or driver to go somewhere

jet bridge (JET BRIJ) an enclosed, movable connector that stretches from an airport gate to an airplane

knots (NAHTS) units of measuring the speed of a ship or an aircraft, equal to 6,076 feet per hour

supersonic (soo-pur-SAH-nik) at or having to do with a speed faster than that of sound

taxi (TAK-see) when planes taxi, they move along the ground before taking off or after landing

turbulence (TUR-byuh-luhns) irregular motion of the atmosphere, marked by sudden gusts and lulls in wind

INDEX

Page numbers in *italics* indicates illustrations.

INDEX *(CONTINUED)*

ABOUT THE AUTHOR

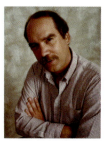

STEVEN OTFINOSKI has written more than 160 books for young readers, including books on the history of television, computers, and rockets. He has also written a biography of helicopter designer Igor Sikorsky. He lives in Connecticut.